# Animal World

# THE PORCUPINE

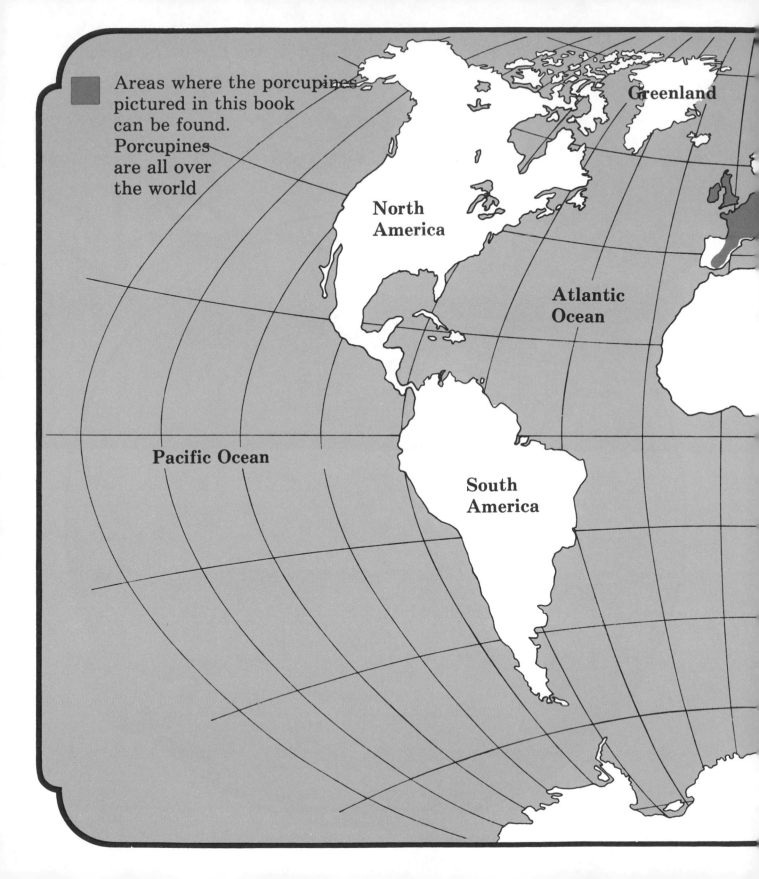

Areas where the porcupines pictured in this book can be found. Porcupines are all over the world

North America

Greenland

Atlantic Ocean

Pacific Ocean

South America

Europe

Asia

Africa

Indian Ocean

Australia

Antarctica

Year 2000 home library edition

Published by The Rourke Enterprises, Inc., P.O. Box 3328, Vero Beach, Florida 32964.
Copyright ©1983 by The Rourke Enterprises, Inc. All copyrights reserved. No part of this
book may be reproduced in any form without written permission from the publisher.
Printed in the United States of America.

**Library of Congress Cataloging in Publication Data**

Dalmais, Anne-Marie, 1954-
  The hedgehog.

  (Animal world)
  Translation of: Le hérisson.
  Reprint: Originally published: London : Macdonald
Educational, 1978.
  Summary: Portrays the Western European hedgehog, a
spiny, solitary creature fond of quiet places.
  1. European hedgehog — Juvenile literature.   [1. Euro-
pean hedgehog.   2. Hedgehogs]   I. Oxenham, Patrick, ill.
II. Title.   III.  Series.
QL737.I53D3413   1984            599.3'3            83-9733
ISBN 0-86592-852-5

# Animal World
# THE PORCUPINE

illustrated by
**Patrick Oxenham**

*This edition produced
exclusively for*
A+ Child Development, Ltd.

ROURKE ENTERPRISES, INC.
Vero Beach, FL 32964

## On the porcupine's trail

A dumpy little figure appears at the end of the garden, in front of the low stone wall. It is an animal with a pointed nose and a coat of sharp spines. It is a porcupine.

You can often see porcupines in the evening when the sun is going down. This is the time when the porcupine usually starts wandering around. It is careful where it goes for its little outings. It has some favorite places. It especially likes quiet spots, away from other animals and people, where it can easily find places to hide. This old, half-crumbling wall and the untidy heap of wood will make an ideal hiding place.

## Mother and young

The porcupine noses around the woodpile, sniffing here and there. After some minutes it darts toward a gap between two stones. It is a mother porcupine and she is returning to her young.

There are five baby porcupines in a nest of leaves. They were born three days ago. Their eyes will stay shut until the fifteenth day. They are covered with soft spines, mostly white but a few of them already colored dull grey. Soon the spines will be brown. They have no hair on their noses or paws.

As the mother suckles them they push against her and make a shrill, squeaking noise. They will stay in the nest for three weeks, cared for by their mother.

## The first outing

The five young porcupines are now three weeks old.
They are bigger and their eyes are wide open. Their
backs bristle with thick brown spines. This evening they
are going into the garden for the first time, under the
watchful eye of their mother.

They leave the nest in a single file. Their noses quiver as they notice all kinds of new smells in the garden. They move with tiny steps, stopping now and then to scratch the ground with their claws.

Soon the hunt for insects is on. One of the porcupines catches a cricket and another gobbles up an earthworm. Until now they have all lived on their mother's milk. For the next week their diet will be a mixed one. They will have milk from their mother, as well as the insects they catch during their outings. After that, they will depend on hunting for all their food.

## Building a nest

When they are two months old, the porcupines leave their mother. Each one goes off on his own to build a nest.

Here you see one of them. He has decided to live in the shelter of a bush. He begins by gathering all the materials he needs and bringing them to the place he has chosen. He finds dead leaves, twigs and dry grass, and he carries them in his mouth. He has to make many journeys.

When he has collected enough of these materials, the porcupine pushes them up into a big heap. Then he rolls around inside the heep to give it a rounded shape.

Not every porcupine's nest is as well made as this. It may be an old rabbit burrow, or a hole in a wall, which the porcupine lines with leaves. Some porcupines take even less trouble. They simply hide in a heap of leaves or oats. It is enough shelter for them.

## The porcupine at dusk

The porcupine sets out every evening at dusk. He sniffs the air first, then he moves off along the garden path.

His legs are short and thin, so he does not move very fast. He pauses quite often to sniff a bit of earth or snap up an insect. His feet make a scrabbling noise on the gravel. Toads and mice get out of his way when they see him coming. They have no wish to be eaten.

The porcupine is on his way to the garden. His path is blocked by a low stone wall which he decides to climb. He grips the wall with his claws, stretches and hoists himself to the top. It is much easier getting down the other side. He just lets himself drop. His spines make a springy cushion for him to fall on.

If you have a porcupine as a pet and you see him falling from a high place, do not be alarmed. He will not hurt himself for he is protected by his spines.

## Food for the porcupine

The porcupine goes on his outings mainly to look for food. He likes to eat insects, slugs, caterpillars, earthworms and snails. He also enjoys frogs, toads, lizards, snakes, fieldmice, birds' eggs, mushrooms and fruit.

Here in the garden, the porcupine smells a beetle in the ground. He digs it up with his claws. Nearby, there is a rabbit nibbling on a turnip.

The porcupine leaves the garden and wanders further on to some fruit trees. On the ground under the trees, he finds plenty of fruit that has fallen from the branches. He sniffs at some apples first, then he munches noisily on some plums. At other times of the year he eats wild gooseberries, blackberries and beech nuts. If it rains, the porcupine cuts the outing short and goes back to his nest.

## Defending himself

Although he is small, the porcupine is not afraid to go out alone at night. He has a very unusual and effective way of defending himself. The moment he feels he is in danger, he rolls his body into a ball and covers himself completely with his spines.

With his armor, he looks just like a pin cushion. Not even a big farm dog will dare to attack him. He can even fight snakes. He brings the spines on his head down like the front piece of a helmet, and on his sides they stick out like a shield. Then he hurls himself at the snake. He attacks several times. Then he seizes the snake in his jaws as close to its head as possible, and snaps its backbone.

Although the porcupine can be harmed by the snake's poison, he does not suffer from a snake bite nearly as badly as a human does. He is also protected against bee stings, and can eat wasps and bumble bees safely.

# Hibernating

When winter comes and the temperature drops, the porcupine rolls himself into a ball and goes to sleep in his nest. Our picture shows the nest with the front part cut away. In real life a porcupine cannot be seen asleep in the nest.

If the weather is not too cold, the porcupine dozes instead of sleeping soundly. He is then easily disturbed by noise.

When the weather becomes very
cold, the porcupine falls into a
deep sleep. He is then said to be
hibernating. His body
temperature falls, but never
below 42°F.

In really severe weather he
wakes up for a time and takes a
short walk out over the snow.
Then he returns to his nest and
goes to sleep again. This can
happen several times during the
winter and the porcupine finds it
extremely tiring.

## Springtime again

With the coming of spring, the porcupine wakes up
completely. The sun shines brightly outside and yellow
daffodils are bursting into flower.

The porcupine carries on as before with outings in the
garden, night raids and his hunt for insects. While he is
out exploring, he chooses a young female for a mate.
Later, she will give birth to a litter of baby porcupines.

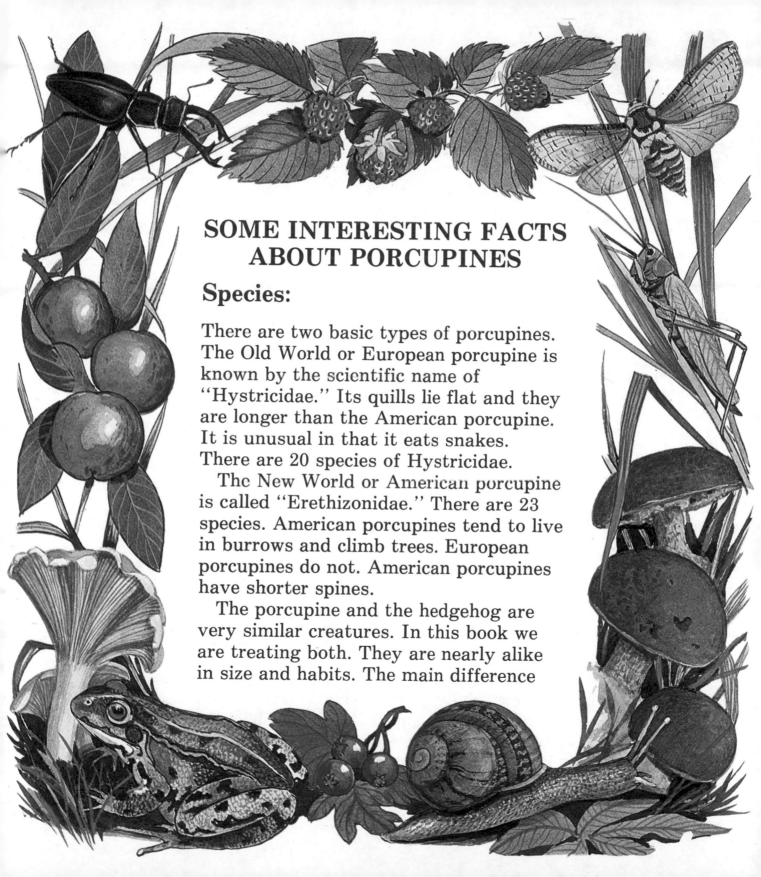

# SOME INTERESTING FACTS ABOUT PORCUPINES

## Species:

There are two basic types of porcupines. The Old World or European porcupine is known by the scientific name of "Hystricidae." Its quills lie flat and they are longer than the American porcupine. It is unusual in that it eats snakes. There are 20 species of Hystricidae.

The New World or American porcupine is called "Erethizonidae." There are 23 species. American porcupines tend to live in burrows and climb trees. European porcupines do not. American porcupines have shorter spines.

The porcupine and the hedgehog are very similar creatures. In this book we are treating both. They are nearly alike in size and habits. The main difference

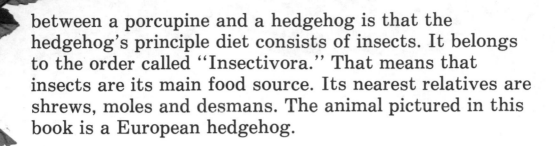

between a porcupine and a hedgehog is that the hedgehog's principle diet consists of insects. It belongs to the order called "Insectivora." That means that insects are its main food source. Its nearest relatives are shrews, moles and desmans. The animal pictured in this book is a European hedgehog.

## Description:

By far, a porcupine's most prominent feature is its spines or quills. One porcupine can have as many as 25,000 spines, some running 20 inches long. They stick out in all directions. The tips are almost white, with bands of brown.

Its spines are also its only means of defense. When an adult porcupine is in danger, it will curl itself into a ball. Most enemies, like the badger and most birds of prey, will give up the fight when this happens. They know that those spines are painful. A spine driven into an enemy may even fester and be fatal. However, some hunters are not so easily put off. Dogs and foxes have been known to push this ball into a lake or pond. When the porcupine hits the water it will open its body to swim. Then it is vulnerable. Then it can be killed.

Spines are also used for attack. The European crested porcupine is especially good at this. It will use its muscles to hold its spines pointed up and back. Then, it will rush backwards at its victim. The spines will stick into the other animal's body.

Despite these moments of aggressiveness, the porcupine is usually calm. It is not very large, only about 9 inches long. Its tail is so small that it can hardly be seen. It is around 9 or 10 inches long. The porcupine weighs between 13 and 21 pounds.

The porcupine has bright eyes, but poor eyesight. It is nearsighted. Its ears are easy to miss, since they are almost covered with fur. The nose is more like a snout. It looks something like a pig's. Its jaws are strong and its teeth are sharp. Its feet are large and flat, with long claws.

The senses of smell and hearing are well developed. A porcupine needs these to catch food. They more than make up for its poor vision. The claws are necessary in climbing trees.

The family of porcupines and hedgehogs are scattered around the world. The crested porcupine, which we mentioned before, is common in Africa and Mediterranean Europe. The Algerian hedgehog lives in northwest Africa and along the coasts of France and Spain. The African brushtailed porcupine is an interesting member of the family. Its tail contains an amazing number of spines. When attacked, the tail acts as a spiny club with which to beat the opponent.

Although you cannot pet them like dogs or cats, some people think that the porcupine makes a good pet. As far back as Roman times, they have been kept for this purpose.

## Family Life:

Old World porcupines tend to nest in grasses or moss. In England, this is called a "hedgerow." They dig tunnels called "warrens." New World, or American porcupines find homes on rocky ledges or hollowed out trees. They like to climb and feed on trees.

A female porcupine is called a "sow." Because porcupines are mammals, the young are born alive and drink milk from their mother's body. A sow has two litters a year. The first group of babies is born in early summer. The second in autumn. There are 3 to 7 babies in a litter. They weigh about one pound at birth. They are blind and helpless. Their backs are covered with soft, pale spines. While they are very young, the mother will move them by carrying them in her mouth. As the weeks pass the spines start to grow and the eyes open.

When a baby porcupine is alarmed it acts in a way that looks strange. Because it is not able to curl into a ball yet it must protect itself in other ways. It jumps up and down to a height of 2 or 3 inches. It keeps on doing this until all danger is passed. A fox or a dog who wants to eat it, would think twice about attacking an excited, spiny animal that is jumping up and down.

Baby porcupines start curling up their bodies when they are about one month old. Also at that time, mother takes them out in search of food.

By the time a baby is 2 months old it leaves home. It is now able to take care of itself. It will spend its days looking under stones for grubs, beetles, caterpillars, snails, frogs, mice and rats. That is the porcupine's basic diet. Some species of porcupines have been known to kill snakes, even poisonous adders. The young porcupine has learned to sleep in the day and hunt at night. An exception to this: porcupines can be seen in the daytime after a rainstorm. Rain brings out the worms and snails that they love. So, they come out to hunt them.

Porcupines have an intense craving for salt. They will eat nearly anything which contains salt. They have even been known to eat hammer and shovel handles which contain salty human sweat.

The porcupine is a hibernating animal. He sleeps during wintertime. Hibernation is more than just sleep, though. The rate of breathing and the pulse both slow down a great deal. The body temperature drops to about 50 degrees F. The metabolism is very slow. At this time the animal lives on the fat which it built up during the year. This fat is now burned away, just fast enough to keep the porcupine alive. If he has not accumulated enough fat, or if it is burned off too fast, the animal will die. Unlike other hibernating animals, porcupines cannot live off a supply of nuts or seeds hidden in its den. Porcupines do not eat that type of food. If it is really hungry, on a warm winter day it will wake up and look for food outside.

An interesting member of the porcupine family is the spiny anteater or echidna. It lives in Australia, Tasmania and New Guinea. It has shorter, stouter spines than the usual porcupine and also curls into a ball. However, the echidna and the platypus are the only two egg-laying mammals still alive today.

## Conservation:

The porcupine has never been in real danger from man. It does not have beautiful fur that can be made into an expensive coat. Few people think that the flesh tastes good. The most trouble it has had is with the automobile. People driving at night do not see them on the road and run them over.

Its other enemies are the fox, the badger, and some birds of prey.

Porcupines tend to be a nuisance to farmers and woodsmen. They will eat parts of a tree and cause the loss of valuable timberland. On the other hand, they are good for farmers because they eat insects which damage crops.